HELPS FOR COUNSELORS

A mini-manual for Christian Counseling

Jay E. Adams

BAKER BOOK HOUSE
Grand Rapids, Michigan

This material is taken from
The Christian Counselor's New Testament

Reprinted 1980 by Baker Book House Company
with the permission of the copyright owner

ISBN: 0-8010-0156-0

Fourth printing, August 1984

PHOTOLITHOPRINTED BY CUSHING - MALLOY, INC.
ANN ARBOR, MICHIGAN, UNITED STATES OF AMERICA

Preface

Helps for Christian Counselors originally was included as a part of *The Christian Counselor's New Testament.* It was designed to be used as a handy reference guide before, after, and during counseling sessions.

This mini-manual presupposes a knowledge of the form of biblical counseling that I set forth in books such as *Competent to Counsel, The Christian Counselor's Manual, Lectures on Counseling,* and *More than Redemption.* Much of the material in this mini-manual is immediately intelligible even without that knowledge, but it will be used most effectively in conjunction with the above-mentioned volumes.

The helps in the mini-manual are intended to be used in preparation for counseling to stimulate planning and review of progress, to help locate significant passages during a counseling session, and to help discover causes of failure. Although they were not designed as study guides, many have found them helpful for such purposes.

In the sections titled Data Gathering (pp. 11-16) and The Counselor's Topical Worklist (pp. 50-61) I have provided space for the counselor to insert additional notations and verse references. The counseling outlines may be used for review and preparation, but also will be a helpful guide to counselors in discussing particular subjects during the actual counseling process. Some have used the outlines in lecturing and preaching. The counselor should keep in mind that the outlines have been simplified for handy reference and therefore, do not cover any topic exhaustively.

I wish to express my appreciation to Baker Book House for suggesting that these helps might be published separately.

JAY ADAMS
The Millhouse, 1979

Counselor's Quick Check List

(*Go over before each counseling session*)

1. Determine whether evangelism is indicated.
2. Sort out responsibilities.
3. Gather concrete data.
4. Stress *what* rather than *why* for data.
5. Distinguish presentation, performance, and presentation problems.
6. Talk not only about problems; talk also about God's solutions.
7. Check motivation (ultimately it must be *loving obedience:* I will do it because God says so, and I want to please Him no matter what).
8. Insist on obedience to God regardless of how one *feels.*
9. Check out Agendas.
10. Give concrete homework at every session. (Explain in detail "how to" assignments; begin with single-stranded problems.)
11. Always check up on homework.
12. Would a medical evaluation be advisable?

Fifty Failure Factors

For a more detailed check on what *may* be behind counseling failure, and also as a guide to correcting mistakes, consider the following factors:

1. Is the counselee truly a Christian?
2. Has there been genuine repentance?
3. Is there a vital commitment to the biblical change?
4. Are your agendas in harmony?
5. Do you have *all* of the necessary data?
6. Are you trying to achieve change in the abstract or concretely?
7. Have you been intellectualizing?
8. Would a medical examination be in order?
9. Are you sure that you know the problem(s)? Is more data gathering necessary?
10. Are there other problems that must be settled first?
11. Have you been trying to deal with the *issue* while ignoring the *relationship?*
12. Did you give adequate scriptural hope?
13. Did you minimize?
14. Have you accepted speculative data as true?
15. Are you regularly assigning concrete homework?
16. Would using a D.P.P. form help?
17. If this is a life-dominating problem, are you counseling for total restructuring?
18. Are you empathizing with self-pity?
19. Are you talking about problems only or also about God's solutions?
20. Have you carefully analyzed the counselee's attitudes expressed in his language?
21. Have you allowed the counselees to talk about others behind their backs?
22. Has a new problem entered the picture, or has the situation changed since the counseling sessions began?
23. Have you been focusing on the wrong problem?
24. Is the problem not so complex after all, but simply a case of open rebellion?
25. Have you failed to move forward rapidly enough in the giving of homework assignments?

26. Have you as a counselor fallen into some of the same problems as the counselee?
27. Does doctrinal error lie at the base of the problem?
28. Do drugs (tranquilizers, etc.) present a complicating problem?
29. Have you stressed the put-off to the exclusion of the put-on?
30. Have you prayed about the problem?
31. Have you personally turned off the counselee in some way?
32. Is he willing to settle for something less than the scriptural solution?
33. Have you been less aggressive and demanding than the Scriptures?
34. Have you failed to give hope by calling sin *sin?*
35. Is the counselee convinced that personality change is impossible?
36. Has your counseling been feeling-oriented rather than commandment-oriented?
37. Have you failed to use the full resources of Christ (e.g., the help of the Christian community)?
38. Is church discipline in order?
39. Have you set poor patterns in previous sessions (e.g., accepting partially fulfilled homework assignments)?
40. Do you really know the biblical solution(s) to his problem? (Can you write it out in thematic form?)
41. Do you really believe there is hope?
42. Has the counselee been praying, reading the Scriptures, fellowshipping with God's people, and witnessing regularly?
43. Could you call another Christian counselor for help (with the counselee's knowledge, of course)?
44. Would a full rereading of your Weekly Counseling Records disclose any patterns? Trends? Unexplored areas?
45. Have you questioned only intensively? Extensively?
46. Have you been assuming (wrongfully) that this case is similar to a previous case?
47. Has the counselee been concealing or twisting data?
48. Would someone else involved in the problem (husband, wife, parent, child) be able to supply needed data?
49. Are you simply incompetent to handle this sort of problem?
50. Are you reasonably sure that there is no organic base to the problem?

Remarks and Responses

Remember, counselees convincingly use language to talk to themselves as well as to talk to others. Therefore, erroneous language must be challenged.

Typical Counselee Remarks	*Typical Counselor Responses That May Be Used*
1. "I can't."	1. "Do you mean can't or won't? God says you *can*.
2. "I've done everything I could."	2. "Everything? What about. . . ."
3. "I've tried that but it didn't work."	3. "Did you *really* try? How many times? For how long? In what way? How consistently?" Get the details: "Precisely, what *did* you do?")
4. "I did my best."	4. "Are you sure? Tell me precisely *what* you did." Or, "Remember, the *best* is what God says to do. Did you . . .?"
5. "*No one* believes me, etc."	5. "Can't you think of *one* person who does? How about some more?" Or, "I believe you."
6. "I could *never* do *that*."	6. "Never is a long time. Really, how long do you suppose it might take to learn? By the way, if you think hard enough, you will discover that you have learned to do a number of things that are just as hard (or harder). For instance, . . ."
7. "If I had the time, I'd do it."	7. "You do. We all have 24 hours hours each day; it all depends on how you slice the pie. Now let's work on drawing up a schedule that honors God."
8. "Don't blame me. . . ."	8. "You're saying you are not responsible? God says. . . ."
9. "Don't ask me. . . ."	9. "But I am asking you. Who else would know? I am sure that you know the answer. Think hard; I'll help you by asking some other related questions, and perhaps we can come up with it."
10. "I guess so."	10. "Are you really guessing or is that what you believe (think)?"
11. "You know how it is. . . ."	11. "No, I don't know; can you explain it more fully?"

Remarks and Responses

Typical Counselee Remarks	*Typical Counselor Responses That May Be Used*
12. "But I've *prayed* about it."	12. "Fine! Then what did you *do?*" Or, "Have you prayed for help to discover what God's Word says to *do* about the problem?" or, "What, exactly, did you pray?"
13. "I'm at the end of my rope."	13. "Which end? Perhaps you are beginning to uncoil your problem for the first time."
14. "I have a need to. . . ."	14. "Is it a need or only a desire? (or, habit)."
15. "I'm just one of those people who has to. . . ."	15. "Yes, I'm sure you are; but Christ wants you to become a different sort of person."
16. "That's just the way I am."	16. "Doubtless, but God says that you can be different."
17. "That is impossible."	17. "You mean it's very difficult."
18. "There are all sorts of [too many] objections to doing that."	18. "Would you mind naming six or seven so that I can see what sort of things you have in mind and determine what it will take to answer them?"
19. "You can't teach an old dog new tricks."	19. "Perhaps that is true—but you are not a dog. You were created in the image and likeness of God! He knows you and commands you to change."
20. "It'll never work."	20. "It is God's way and it *always* works when people abandon that attitude."
21. "I'll never forgive him!"	21. "If you are a child of God, as you claim, you will. You are going to live with him for eternity; why not forgive him and begin to get used to it now?"
22. "I don't do anything half way, so. . . ."	22. "You're sure? Can't you think of some things that you do? For instance, what about . . .?"
23. "Everything[one] is against me. . . ."	23. "No, you are wrong. If you are a Christian, the Bible says the opposite: 'If God be for us, who can be against us?' (Rom. 8:31)."
24. "How do you feel about . . .?"	24. "May I tell you what I think, or may I only discuss my emotions?"

Data Gathering

An important aspect of counseling is data gathering. The following four helps will be found useful in collecting data. When you know what motivates people to seek counseling, what problems are common to various classes of persons, how to discover where their major known difficulties lie, and how to uncover unknown data, your effectiveness to help counselees will increase greatly. Each of the helps that follow is designed to do each of these things.

Why People Come for Counseling

It is important to distinguish among the varous problems that motivate persons to seek help. The following list, while not exhaustive, may aid. It includes twenty of the most frequent reasons why persons seek counselors.

1. Advice in making simple decisions
2. Answers to troublesome questions
3. Depression and guilt
4. Guidance in determining careers
5. Breakdowns
6. Crises
7. Failures
8. Grief
9. Bizarre behavior
10. Anxiety, worry, and fear
11. Other unpleasant feelings
12. Family and marital trouble
13. Help in resolution of conflicts with others
14. Deteriorating interpersonal relations
15. Drug and alcohol problems
16. Sexual difficulties
17. Perceptual distortions
18. Psychosomatic problems
19. Attempted suicide
20. Difficulties at work or school

It is important to know in what areas problems are likely to lie.

With various classes of persons, special areas ordinarily (perhaps *usually*) contain the "hot spots."

With *children,* counselors should look for problems in child/parent relations, peer-group difficulties, and teacher and school tensions.

With *older children and singles,* in addition to some of the above, explore the possibility of sexual difficulties, dating problems, communication breakdown, trouble with life-meaning, the discovery, development and use of gifts, and school and/or work.

With *older singles,* look especally for resentment over failure to marry and explore objectionable habit patterns that may have become obstructions to and reduce one's marriage potential. Look for possible homosexual or lesbian problems. Check up on disorganization of life schedules.

With *married persons,* investigate not only strains arising from the marriage itself, but from the family's relationship to in-laws, problems relating to work or homemaking, financial worries, and the discipline of children. Communication breakdown, resentment, and depression are all possibilities too.

Older persons may suffer from loneliness, self-pity, physical aches and pains, time wastage, purposelessness, and the fear of death.

Handicapped persons also present specialized problems. In particular, look for resentment (against God and/or others), loneliness, and self-pity. A sense of uselessness may prevail. Such persons need to be shown how to thank God for problems and how to turn their liabilities into assets by the grace of God. Often the handicapped counselee has developed patterns in which he has learned to use his handicap to manipulate others around him.

Not all of these problems are always present in each case. In some instances the special factors that characterize an individual in a particular category may play no part in the problem at all. Yet, even where some other problem or problems not specifically related to age, or singleness, or marriage, etc., seem to dominate, the special problems within the category may form secondary or complicating problems (e.g., "I know why we had the argument; I'm old and useless and just in everyone's way"), and will have to be dealt with as well.

Extensive Questioning

In data gathering, remember to ask *what* type questions rather than *why* type questions. The former are more likely to elicit facts, the latter speculation. In gathering data, if possible, always begin with extensive rather than intensive questioning.

In this approach the counselor uses the shotgun rather than the rifle. He sprays questions like shot across the whole gamut of life. The counselor may wish to open the helps to the following list when doing extensive counseling. Space has been provided for adding one's own additional questions. The list is suggestive, not exhaustive. Ask about:

1. *The counselee's relationship to God;* to the church. Is he saved, is there guilt over particular sins, what are his life goals, have there been any significant changes in these areas lately?

2. *His habits* of Scripture reading and study, prayer, Christian service, use of gifts, witnessing.

3. *His relationship to others:* wife/husband, father/mother, children, in-laws (especially the wife's mother-in-law or a daughter-in-law), neighbors, relatives, other significant persons.

4. *His work (or school work):* does he enjoy it, have problems with it, is he afraid of failure, does he do an adequate job? What about his relationship to others there? Any recent changes at work?

5. *His physical life:* adequate exercise, sleep (remember the effects of significant sleep loss), and diet; about illnesses, injuries, or bodily abuses. What about the sexual life?

6. *His financial affairs:* does he tithe and give to the church, pay bills, budget the funds, pay taxes faithfully? Does his/her spouse and he/she argue over money? Any recent financial setbacks?

7. *Social and recreational.* Adequate? Family, husband/wife outings, vacations, dates, friends?

8. *Time:* organized, disorganized? Priorities right before God? Schedule? Behind?

9. Have there been any *tragedies, deaths, crises, major life changes recently,* in last half year, in last year?

10. Is there *fear, anger, bitterness and resentment, depression, guilt* or other bad feelings, attitudes?

These questions are supplemental to those asked on the Personal Data Inventory, and are not intended to replace them. Some are repetitious, but it is often necessary to ask a question more than once in different contexts.

As the counselor checks out these areas, he makes a careful record of responses (recording both core and halo data), asking further questions that grow out of feedback, but never allowing the checkout to become bogged down in any one area. In the agenda column, the counselor makes notations of all the areas that he will want to investigate more intensively later on. These include areas in which core data indicate certain or possible problems and where halo data (nervousness, body movements, unusual tension, stuttering, surprise, embarrassment, regret, evasion, etc.) seem to indicate particular sensitivity.

Discovering Problem Patterns

Patterns are not always known to the counselee and may not immediately become apparent to the counselor. The use of a D.P.P. Form may be assigned as homework for one to four weeks to help uncover such patterns. The form has been designed for simplicity of use by the counselee. A sample follows:

Name ....

Date ....

Directions: For one week carefully list *all* events, situations or activities (good or bad) that resulted in ....
Circle those that occur three or more times.

	Sun.	Mon.	Tues.	Wed.	Thur.	Fri.	Sat.
Morning							
Afternoon							
Evening							

The D.P.P. is a flexible instrument. For instance, if a counselee is concerned about breaking a pattern of eating between meals, he may keep a D.P.P. to determine when he eats (or desires to). He may discover from this that eating is connected with certain situations such as (1) when watching TV, (2) when concerned about the children, (3) when under stress, (4) just before supper when hungry. Gathering such data is useful for mapping out a strategy for breaking and replacing the habit. In interpreting the D.P.P., look for recurring events (situations) or periods (time). The pattern may be geographical, chronological, interpersonal, etc. The form is available in the *Christian Counselor's Starter Packet* or in any quantity from the publisher.

Question Asking

I. Begin with the three basics (all *what* type questions). These are a summary of the questions asked by Christ and the apostles.
   A. Q. 1.—What is your problem? (Three levels of responses).
      1. Irritation level—"I'm depressed."
      2. Particular instance—"I'm depressed because I had a brawl with my mother-in-law."
      3. Underlying pattern—"I'm depressed because I had a brawl like I always do when I lose my cool.
   B. Q. 2.—What have you done about it?
      1. Further complicated matters in the attempts to solve it.
      2. Failed to realize that other matters are even more serious (e.g., the *relationship* must be healed before the solution to the *issue* is possible).
   C. Q. 3.—What do you want me to do?
      1. Agenda problem—be sure that you both want the same thing: God's will.
      2. Basic motivation to please God (not to get wife back, get relief from the misery, etc.; all else is secondary.

II. Seek data
   A. Stress *what* type questions (to elicit facts) rather than *why* type questions (that evoke speculation).
   B. Do not ask questions that can be answered by yes/no. (Save those for commitment.)
   C. Let subsequent questions grow from previous answers.
      1. As in normal conversations.

2. With this exception: you have been invited to ask more personal questions (but there still are limits).

D. Ask questions from extensive and intensive approaches.

E. Watch for nonverbal halo data.

F. Ask for exact, concrete specifics; do not settle for generalizations or abstractions.

Listening

There is much information about the value and the place of listening in counseling. While listening is a vital aspect of counseling, remember that it is only one aspect. It must never be equated with counseling as if it were the all-in-all or even the most important aspect of the work. Listening is *one* essential means to the counselor's ends.

I. God says: Listen for *facts* (Prov. 18:13).

A. Don't jump to conclusions (e.g., appearances deceive).

1. The first problem raised may not be the most basic one.
2. It may have been offered as a trial balloon to see how you handle problems.

B. One reason for the failure suggested: the counselor may be too anxious to speak.

1. He may offer a few pat answers (solutions) for everything, or his problem may be
2. Stereotyping (failure to recognize true diversity), or
3. Failure to distinguish things that differ but look alike:
   a. Bizarre behavior from sleep loss; from organic causes.
   b. Tendency to identify with a recent success: "Looks just like the case I handled last week," or
4. Failure to distinguish the three levels of response to the question, "What is your problem?"

C. You need to gather facts:

1. God doesn't stress the value of listening per se in this passage,

2. But the value of listening as a means for obtaining data about which to speak.
3. Verse 13 (and 15) pictures a data-gathering situation.

D. The passage does not imply that no response, no advice will be given, but rather
 1. That, contrary to Carl Rogers,
 2. Listening is to gather data that will enable one to answer and advise properly.
 3. These verses are not problem-focused, but solution-oriented.

II. Listen *actively* for the facts (Prov. 18:15).
 A. The listener is pictured not passively but actively listening
  1. To *acquire* knowledge,
  2. By *seeking* it.
 B. The data needed to give an appropriate answer do not come from listening
  1. To stream-of-consciousness talk structured by the counselee,
  2. But to talk elicited by and structured by the counselor.
 C. The counselor must control the flow of talk.
  1. He seeks and finds data he is looking for as well as those data that the counselee wishes to offer.
  2. He is prudent and wise in the way in which he conducts the data-gathering sessions.
   a. He knows what to ask,
   b. When to ask it,
   c. And how to word his questions (see material on question asking).
 D. He listens for facts, not merely for attitudes and feelings.
  1. Notice, he seeks "knowledge" or "information."
  2. Notice further, feeling is not once mentioned in these verses.

III. Listen for *all* of the facts (Prov. 18:17).
 A. There are two or more sides to many issues:

1. This implies that all parties should be present if possible,
2. That each should hear what the other says in order to explain, modify, amplify, etc. (note "examine"),
3. And it is clear that one must not be allowed to speak negatively about another behind his back (see also James 4:11).

B. The first to speak can sound quite convincing if heard alone,
1. But the additional information that the other provides can turn the conclusion about face.
2. As, for instance, when one counselee said,
"He hit me! He slapped me in the face!"
And her husband replied:
"Sure, to bring her to her senses. She was hysterically screaming and beating herself on the head with her fists."

Homework

Homework enables the counselor to do more counseling more rapidly. Written homework speeds up counseling. Work is not confined to the counseling session alone. Indeed, work continues throughout the week. Counseling does not sag, then, in between the sessions. Actually, homework emphasizes the important fact that most of the work must be done by the counselee outside of the counseling session itself. Change with respect to one's job or neighbors or relatives does not take place within the sessions themselves. The work has to be done outside, and that is what the counseling assignment focuses upon. Compare the following:

Fig. One

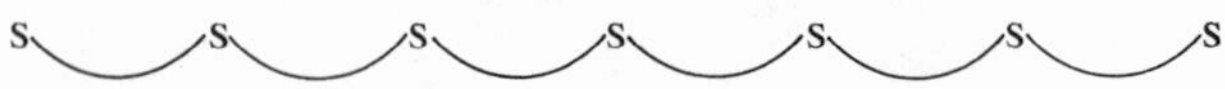

A focus upon the counseling session(s) causes a sag during the intervening periods. Approaches that emphasize the session as the magic hour tend to (1) stress the expert, (2) fail to get much done quickly, and (3) make counselees dependent upon the counselor.

Fig. Two

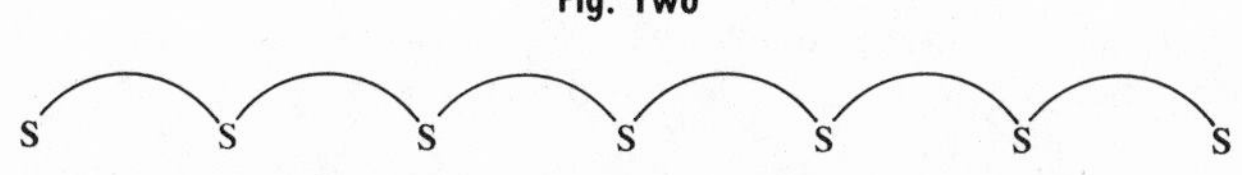

A focus upon the week's work (1) makes the counselee's relationship to God and his neighbor (rather than to the counselor) most significant, (2) stresses life as it is lived rather than the magic hour, and (3) gets much done quickly by daily effort rather than dependence upon a one-hour weekly session.

I. Use homework
   A. Every week
   B. Beginning with the first session.

II. Set pattern of expectation of change from the outset ("You can be different today").
   A. Not everything can be done at once.
   B. But start with some homework to make some change.
   C. Something can always be done.

III. Homework brings hope from the outset.
   A. Something is happening.
   B. Even small advances are advances; sometimes they make great changes in outlook.

IV. Homework allows you to discover quickly who means business and who does not.
   A. Cf. Matthew 19:16ff.: the rich young ruler who got the toughest assignment of all.
   B. Homework reveals sin; often brings conviction.

V. Written homework keeps expectations clear.
   A. Counselees are often emotionally excited in sessions; miss points, misinterpret.
   B. Keeps down arguments between spouses, etc.

C. Homework book reminds of work to be done throughout the week.

VI. Homework enables you to do more work more rapidly.
  A. Work not confined to sessions.
  B. Counselee can gather data in one week what it might have taken five or six sessions to uncover.

VII. Homework keeps down dependency.
  A. Focus is upon the environment in which the changes must occur
  B. Rather than upon the session as the "magic hour."
  C. Puts responsibility upon the counselee to change before God and neighbor.

VIII. Allows patterns and problems to emerge
  A. Naturally, under current, controlled conditions.
  B. Uncovers problems unknown to counselee before.

IX. Homework becomes a yardstick for measuring progress.
  A. Easy to deceive oneself as to progress (or lack of it).
  B. Easy for both counselor/counselee to deceive themselves.

X. Homework at the end of counseling.
  A. Provides a personalized workbook for future reference.
  B. Is a reminder to assure against future failure.
  C. Keeps counselee from necessity to return to counselor.

Assigning Lists for Homework

Among those lists that counselors find useful to assign as homework are these:

1. Lists of one's own sins (then, after taking the log out of his own eye, a list of another's).
2. List of strengths, gifts, abilities, and skills.
3. List of small things to do to please another (one for each day).
4. List of the directions given in the book of James.
5. List of purposes and goals in life.
6. List of at least twenty ways in which God blessed you during the week.
7. List as many ways as you can of putting another first (cf. Phil. 2:3, 4).

8. List of ways to overcome evil with good (cf. Rom. 12: 14-21).
9. List of things you strongly desire, but cannot have.
10. List of "If . . . , then" excuses you habitually make.
11. List of unbiblical proverbs, unscriptural language, contrary to the Bible, that have become a part of your vocabulary and thinking.
12. List of matters that are troubling you at the moment.

A Sample List

(abbreviated, with counselors notations)

about what? Ask for specifics (remember can't change abstractly)

HIS	*HER*
1. I snore and this annoys my wife. *Was he serious, or a bit uncooperative in making this entry?*	1. I do not trust Fred as I should. *too general (get specifics – about what?) Too large for early sessions*
2. I do not lead family devotions. *Good to work on right away.*	2. I try to push Fred into things. *Get details here: What things? For what reasons?*
3. I clam up. *Work on soon (2nd or 3rd session)*	3. I nag him incessantly. *Work on in combination with his #3*
4. I haven't finished small jobs around house. *Good opening assignment if you can get sub list.*	4. I yell at children. *Connect with Fred's #5.*
5. I fail to discipline children as I should. *(Again, get specifics – then work on code of conduct)*	5. I do not keep the house in order. *Get specifics; these are high priority items for first assignments.*
6. I am inconsiderate of Barbara's feelings. *(Again, in what ways? – possible first assignments if you get specifics)*	6. I am jealous. *Ask Fred straight out: "Is there any basis for this?"*

Homework

HIS	HER
7. I work too late at night. *Connect with Barbara's #11*	7. I have a hard time making decisions. *Ask for 3 or 4 examples*
8. I blame things on Barbara that are my fault. *Get a half dozen examples*	8. I lose my temper. *Work on at later point. At 1st session, give her a DPP to determine what occasions it.*
9. I hardly ever express my ideas clearly or fully. *Explore in depth later on.*	9. I forget to tell Fred about phone messages. *good, Concrete. Work on agreed upon method for solving. Chalk-board on wall?*
10. I want things done my way or not at all. *— Ask for examples.*	10. I take over leadership of home. *Will require full discussion later. Connect with Fred's #2, 5, 7. Assign appropriate chapters in Christian Living in the Home for both*
11. Barbara is too involved with children; doesn't care about me. *Explore in depth at some early session.*	11. Fred shows attention to other women. *Check out connection with #1 & 6.*
12. Barbara is too fussy about way boys cut grass.	12. He is not home enough. *get exact data on. Keep weekly schedule on hours home.*
13. She often refuses to have sexual relations. *Place on agenda for later discussion and work*	13. Fred is dull and uninteresting. *Ask: "How would you like him to be?" Later assign Barbara task of describing the kind of man she would like to see him become.*
14. She is thoughtless. *Give examples*	14. He has given up on the marriage. *What leads you to say this?*
15. Barbara's mother meddles in our family. *— put on agenda*	

Counseling Outlines

The following outlines summarize the teaching on various subjects as they have been developed from the Scriptures in my books, *Competent to Counsel* and *The Christian Counselor's Manual*. They are neither exhaustive nor complete.[1] The purpose of these summary outlines is to provide guidelines for rapid review before or during a counseling session. Some counselors will find it helpful to open to the outline that summarizes a key portion of biblical teaching on a given topic when they are about to discuss that topic with a counselee. Since they are intended to be used in such situations, the outlines are kept simple and uncluttered. The counselor may wish to fill in the outlines with additional points, Scripture references, and illustrations. The subjects have been arranged alphabetically

[1] The counselor would be wise to reread each section in *Competent* and in the *Manual* for further insights.

ANGER

I. Anger is not sinful in itself.
   A. It is an emotion designed to mobilize force to tear something apart.
   B. Cf. Psalm 7:11; Mark 3:5.
   C. Ephesians 4:26 indicates that its expression may be sinful.

II. Anger is sinful
   A. When it grows out of pride, hurt feelings, etc.
   B. When it is expressed in sinful ways.

III. Two sinful expressions of righteous anger are
   A. Blowing up (ventilation).
      1. Proverbs 29:11; 25:28; Ephesians 4:31.
      2. Energy is wasted and used to tear up others.
   B. Clamming up (internalization).
      1. Leviticus 19:17, 18; Ephesians 4:26.
      2. Energy is wasted and used to tear up self.

IV. There is a scripturally acceptable expression of anger.
   A. Not the opposite extreme of either sinful one:
      1. Internalization to ventilation, or
      2. Ventilation to internalization,
   B. But anger released under control and aimed at tearing up the problem while building up persons (Eph. 4:29).

BIZARRE BEHAVIOR

Avoid labels that point toward uncertainties (e.g., schizophrenic, psyhcotic). There are various possible causes of bizarre behavior; treat each case separately. The same behavior can be caused by widely different factors (e.g., hallucinations may come from sleep loss, L.S.D., fever, chemical malfunction within the body, etc.). There are two basic causes of bizarre behavior that are not necessarily unrelated:

BIZARRE BEHAVIOR

ORGANIC CAUSES	NONORGANIC CAUSES
Perceptual Problems Hallucinogenic Drugs Malfunctioning of Bodily Chemistry Sleep Loss	Camouflage Mind Sets that distort reality
Brain Damage Injury Tumor Toxic Reactions	Life Patterns Conscience triggering fear and/or other bodily reactions or malfunctions.
Other	
And, possible combinations of each.	

CHANGE

I. God demands change (Eph. 4:17)
   A. From feeling-motivated living
   B. To commandment-motivated living.

II. God effects this change by renewing the image ruined by the fall (Eph. 4:20-24).
   A. The Holy Spirit has been given to renew us.
   B. This renewal is in knowledge, righteousness, and holiness (cf. Col. 3:5-11).

III. God effects the change by enabling us
   A. To put off the old man:
      1. The former manner of life;
      2. Our habitual response patterns.
   B. To put on the new man:
      1. New biblical manner of life;
      2. New habitual patterns to replace the old.

IV. God provides scriptural alternatives.
   A. Change is two-factored:
      1. Not breaking habits alone,
      2. But also replacing them.
   B. Counselors must focus on both.
   C. Examples of alternatives:
      1. Lying/Speaking the truth (Eph. 4:25).
      2. Returning evil/Returning good (I Pet. 3:9).
   D. Counselor's task:
      1. To discover the biblical alternatives;
      2. To help counselee to replace old patterns with the new ones.

DEPRESSION

I. The counselee must recognize his responsibility for depression.
   A. From time to time all of us get down (II Cor. 4:8).
      1. But this is not depression.
      2. Depression is ceasing to function in our daily chores and interests (giving up on responsibilities).
   B. When we get down we do not need to be out.
   C. Depression is when one is both down and out.

II. Depression results from handling a down period sinfully.
   A. We get down (blue, discouraged, etc.) from both sinful causes (guilt) and non-sinful causes (sickness, financial reverses, etc.),
   B. But when we give in to down feelings
      1. We let chores and interests slide;
      2. We then feel even less like doing them and brood instead,
      3. Thus increasing our guilt from failure to achieve,
      4. And this makes us feel less like doing things, and we spiral downward into a depression.

III. Counselees may spiral up out of depression
   A. By asking God's forgiveness;
   B. By doing chores and assuming responsibilities;
   C. And by similarly dealing with any other matter of guilt.

IV. Counselees can stay out of depression
   A. By following God's commands when down, rather than following their feelings;
   B. By carefully scheduling and following the schedule no matter how they feel;
   C. By avoiding pity parties and refusing to engage in brooding;
   D. By repenting of any sin immediately;
   E. By immediately straightening out any relationship to God or man that goes sour;
   F. And by changing all erroneous vocabulary (by which they convince themselves that "things are hopeless" or "I can't take it any more," etc.).

OVERCOMING EVIL
(Romans 12:14-21)

I. God expects counselees to overcome evil (vs. 21)
   A. Not only to be undefeated (do not be overcome with evil),
   B. But also to defeat evil (overcome evil with good).

II. God expects these battles to be fought and won His way: with good.
   A. Evil is a popgun; good is an atomic weapon. God will not allow the use of weak weapons.
   B. When persecuted, the counselee is to bless, not curse (vs. 14).
      1. Blessing=asking God to do good for another and saying good things to him yourself.
      2. Cursing=asking God to damn him and saying evil things to him yourself.
   C. Do concrete good toward an enemy (vs. 20):
      1. Something to eat, a drink, or whatever the counselee has that will meet his needs.
      2. The counselee does this out of love for God, whether he feels like it or not.

III. Counselees must never pay back evil for evil (vs. 17).
   A. Love does not retaliate.
      1. Fools do this (Prov. 26:4, 5), and thus only spread more evil
      2. And become like the fool who did evil to begin with.
   B. Instead, respect (literally, *plan*) what is good in the sight of all.
      1. You won't do good otherwise; you must prepare for the crisis ahead of time
      2. By hard work, much thought, and prayer.

IV. Counselees must seek peace with everyone (vs. 18)—believers, unbelievers
   A. Although it is not always possible to achieve.
   B. Nevertheless, they must act responsibly so that *they* do everything they can to see that peace is secure; any

failure must not be on *their* side of the relationship.

C. That means that counselees
   1. Must not *provoke* trouble;
   2. Must not *protract* (widen, extend) trouble (cf. Prov. 15:1);
   3. Must not *prolong* trouble (cf. Eph. 4:26; Matt. 5:23, 24; Luke 18:15ff.).

V. Counselees must never take revenge (vs. 19).

A. God Himself will avenge.
   1. That is His job; He has not allowed us to do it
   2. So step aside and make room for God to step in when and how He pleases.

B. He promises to repay
   1. Perhaps in His Son, who suffered for the sins of those who will believe.
   2. In eternal wrath upon those who will refuse to believe (II Thess. 1:6-8).
   3. And in His own fatherly ways even with believers (I Thess. 4:6).

VI. Counselees are to subdue enemies by their expression of love.

A. They are to heap coals upon their heads.
   1. Picture shovelling hot coals over a hillside onto an enemy's head.
   2. Rough warfare (equivalent of modern flame thrower) successfully subdues him.

B. God's own method for subduing His enemies: Romans 2:4; 5:8, 10.

C. Cf. the way a Christian wife is instructed to win her unsaved husband (I Pet. 3:1ff.).

FEAR

I. The counselee must recognize that fear is a good safety emotion
   A. That keeps us from falling off cliffs, etc.,
   B. And that alerts us to other dangers, even in human relationships.

II. But he also must see that the emotion can be perverted.
   A. By fearing what God forbids,
   B. And by failing to follow God's commands out of fear.

III. The counselee must understand how fear works:
   A. A fear (panic) experience is highly unpleasant
   B. So that one who has had it *fears* having it again (thereby unwittingly producing it himself).
      1. Phobias attach fear experiences to bridges, elevators, or wherever they were experienced,
      2. So that merely thinking of crossing a bridge, etc., turns into *fear* of crossing it for *fear* of another *fear* experience.
      3. All of which means that the fear of fear is the beginning of fear.

IV. The counselee must learn that only the power of love can overcome fear (I John 4:18).
   A. A mother, afraid of mice, will stand between a tiger and her child out of love.
   B. And a fearful person can do God's will out of love for Him.
   C. Love is keeping God's commandments; thus the keeping of God's commandments is the route to the elimination of fear.

V. The counselee can overcome fear
   A. Not by trying to stop the fear experience from occurring,
   B. But by focusing all his concern upon doing the loving thing for God/neighbor that he has been neglecting out of fear.
      1. This is the biblical alternative,
      2. And when he follows it and becomes so filled with

what he will do in love, there is no time or place for fear.

C. He must be willing to say, "Let the fear experience occur if it will; I'll not fight it. Instead, I shall do as God wishes. And I'll not worry about the possibility of it; I have too much to take up my mind in planning and executing what God wants me to do."

REMEMBER: THE FEAR OF GOD (WHICH MEANS LOVING AND RESPECTFUL OBEDIENCE TOWARD HIM) IS THE ONE FEAR THAT ELIMINATES ALL OTHERS.

FORGIVENESS
(Luke 17:3-10)

I. Jesus says that the counselee must be willing to forgive.
   A. He must grant forgiveness whenever a brother says that he repents.
   B. He must do so as often as he says that he repents (7 times a day).

II. Jesus accepts no excuses for failing to forgive.
   A. Not "when he shows fruit appropriate to repentance."
      1. Not required for granting brotherly forgiveness.
      2. Seven times a day precludes the idea.
      3. Must take him at his word: If he *says,* "I repent." Can judge words and actions; not heart. Give benefit of the doubt.
   B. Not "when I get more faith."
      1. Not a matter of more faith; a question of obedience.
      2. A faith as small as a mustard seed can do wonders.
   C. Not "when I feel like it."
      1. Slave tired and hungry.
      2. Didn't feel like preparing and serving meal before resting and eating.
      3. Did anyway, because his lord commanded.
      4. Not hypocrisy to obey God against feeling (you do this when you get up in the morning). Do against feeling, to please God.

III. Jesus says forgive because He commands it.
   A. Forgive out of love for Christ.
   B. Forgiveness is a promise that can be made and kept regardless of fruit, faith, or feeling. The promise: "I will remember your sins against you no more."
   C. The promise involves three things:
      1. I won't raise these matters with you again.
      2. I won't tell others about them.
      3. I won't dwell on them in my own mind.
   D. Keeping this promise leads to forgetting.

REMEMBER: WHEN YOU FORGIVE, EACH OFFENSE IS NOT THE SEVENTH, FIFTH, ETC.; IT IS ALWAYS THE FIRST.

WE FORGIVE BECAUSE WE ARE FORGIVEN PEOPLE. HOW MANY TIMES GOD HAS FORGIVEN US!

GIFTS

I. Gifts are gifts, not rewards.
   A. They are not the result of holiness;
   B. The church at Corinth, notorious for its unholiness, abounded in gifts (I Cor. 1:7).
   C. Gifts are sovereignly dispensed by the Holy Spirit "as He wills" (I Cor. 12:11b).

II. Every Christian has gifts (Eph. 4:7; I Pet. 4:10; I Cor. 12:11).
   A. But they differ.
   B. They differ in kind, purpose, results, and measure (I Cor. 12:4-6, 11; Eph. 4:7).

III. Individual gifts are given to each one for the benefit of the whole:
   A. I Corinthians 12:7, 14-31.
   B. All are equally important and needed by the whole body (I Cor. 12:11b).

IV. Each Christian should cultivate his gifts for the whole
   A. By discovering them, developing them, and deploying them.
   B. Romans 12:3-7 gives the framework for doing so:
      1. Vs. 3—*evaluate* soberly to discover God's gifts. Examine, test, consult with others, etc.
      2. Vss. 4, 5—*recognize* the function of each gift among the many.
      3. Vss. 6, 7—*use* the gift in practical applications by God's help.

V. The above facts have practical implications for counseling:
   A. Help counselees to stop trying to do what they do not have the gifts to do.
   B. Help counselees to discover, develop, and then to live up to the potential that the measure of their gifts requires.
   C. Help counselees to find the proper place for the exercise of their gifts.
   D. Help counselees to use gifts for the benefit of their

brethren in harmony with them.

E. Help counselees to be thankful for their gifts and not to complain about the Spirit's judgment in not dispensing different ones to them.

F. Help counselees not to complain about others when their efforts are limited by the measure of their gifts.

G. Help counselees not to be proud of their accomplishments, recognizing that the gifts that enabled them to succeed are from God, not from themselves.

GRIEF

I. Grief is a proper expression of emotion.
   A. Jesus grieved at Lazarus' grave (John 11:33-38).
   B. I Thessalonians 4:13 indicates the propriety of grief for the Christian.
   C. Grief is the expression of a painful sorrow:
      1. Word means *pain;* sorrow over a loss that hurts.
      2. It is a life-shattering sorrow coming also from the disruption of old living patterns.
   D. Grief from *loss* of persons (death or separation), position, or power.

II. Grief becomes sinful when it drifts into despair.
   A. The despair that Lindemann and others describe is what happens to unbelievers.
   B. But the believer should grieve differently (I Thess. 4:13).
      1. Hope is an anchor that can keep him from drifting into despair.
      2. He must trust in God and His providential working.
      3. He may know joy in sorrow, knowing the blessings of death to God's children.

III. Grief rarely manifests itself as a simple emotion:
   A. Often complicated by presence of other emotions like fear, anger, resentment, worry, and the feeling of guilt.
   B. Grief also can lead to other complicating problems like sleep loss, depression, etc.

IV. The grief process has three stages:
   A. Initial shock (if not expected).
      1. Could last from a few minutes to a few hours.
      2. Largely comfort (standing by) needed at this point.
      3. Sinful reactions (words, etc.) should be noted and dealt with later on.
   B. Disorganization.
      1. Could last for several weeks; set up regular weekly counseling sessions.
      2. Old patterns in shambles.
         a. Can't go on as in past; change in life style inevit-

able though unwelcome.

b. Past may catch up and come to surface.

c. Time to review old patterns and confess wrongs to God/others.

d. Deal with all complicating problems (see III); sinful reactions.

e. Help counselee clear the rubble of the past (can't build new future life on uncleared rubble).

4. Advise against hasty decisions and significant changes during this period:
   a. To sell house,
   b. To move in to live with children,
   c. To move from community, friends, etc.

C. Reorganization.
   1. May last for several weeks.
   2. Counseling continues:
      a. Opportunity to help to reorganize life afresh,
      b. In ways that will better please Christ than former ones did.
   3. Goal: seize the opportunity to help the counselee to make crucial life decisions for Christ:
      a. Such decisions reserved until this point.
      b. Look for new potentials for service.
      c. Help set objectives and short-term goals.
      d. Help to reorganize life patterns according to biblical principles and priorities.

THE ABC's OF DEALING WITH GUILT

The counselee must

I. *A—Acknowledge* his guilt
   A. In biblical terms: sin against God; not sickness/alienation, etc.
   B. That sin is first against God; then against others (not merely horizontal).

II. *B—Blame* no one but himself:
   A. Not his parents.
   B. Not his spouse.
   C. Not his church.
   D. Not society.
   E. Not God.

III. *C—Confess* his sin
   A. To God, seeking forgiveness (I John 1:7-10).
   B. To any others he may have offended.

INFERIORITY, INADEQUACY

I. Not a feeling
   A. But a judgment: "I judge myself to be inferior (inadequate, etc.)," leading to bad feelings.
   B. Therefore, it can be dealt with (can't turn feelings off).
      1. Because the facts of the judgment can be examined
      2. And appropriate action can be taken in accordance with those facts.

II. The judgment first must be investigated
   A. To see if it is sound.
   B. If it is not, then the counselee must be led to discover this,
   C. Since, when he does, the bad feelings that were triggered by the judgment will leave.

III. If the judgment is a sound one
   A. Based upon facts,
   B. The situation must be discussed to determine whether or not the counselee ought to be anything other than inferior in this way. (He may want to be or do what his gifts will not permit.)
   C. If he ought not to be anything other than inferior in this matter, he must be shown that this is so by consideration of his priorities, his gifts, the rightness of it, etc.

IV. If he is inferior in something in which he ought to excel,
   A. He must be brought to recognize this fact,
   B. And be helped to lay out a plan for achieving the skills/knowledge, etc., needed,
   C. And to learn how to pursue that plan to its fruition,
   D. In God's way, by His strength.

MARRIAGE BASICS

I. God ordained marriage.
   A. Marriage not optional, not an expedient or primarily a civil contract.
   B. God Himself ordained marriage as the first institution of society.
   C. Marriage is a covenantal relationship (cf. Prov. 2:17; Mal. 2:14): THE COVENANT OF COMPANIONSHIP.
      1. From God.
      2. The most serious form of relationship of all (like salvation, which is a covenantal relationship with God).
   D. Marriage is good:
      1. Some speak disparagingly of marriage; extol celibacy,
      2. But God said it is "not good" to be alone (Gen. 2:18).
      3. Celibacy is not higher (I Cor. 7 describes the exception: celibacy is *better* only in a time of persecution). Some singled out by God (Matt. 19).
      4. Marriage is not tainted by sex (cf. Heb. 13:4; Eph. 5:21-33; Rev. 19, the marriage of the spotless lamb).

II. God ordained marriage for His purposes:
   A. To represent the relationship of Christ to His church.
   B. The most basic need met in marriage is companionship (cf. Prov. 2:17; Mal. 2:14—the companion of your youth). Meets man's problem of loneliness (Gen. 2:18).
   C. This companionship provides for
      1. *Help* for the man (Gen. 2:18: "I will make him a helper").
      2. *Complementation and enrichment* of one's life (Gen. 2:18: "who is appropriate to" or "who corresponds to." Together, man and woman make a complete whole physically, intellectually, emotionally).
      3. *Propagation and rearing of children* (Gen. 1:28).

III. God ordained marriage to provide for separate decision-making units: families (Gen. 2:24).

A. The man must leave his parents, making a clean break with the past,
B. And he must cleave to his wife, forming a new unit directly responsible to God.
C. Parents must be willing to have the leaving occur and must encourage it,
D. And children must effect it whether parents are prepared for it or not.

SEXUAL PRINCIPLES

The following list of principles largely grows out of an exposition of I Corinthians 7:1-6. Where other references also have been included, they are cited.

1. Sexual relations within marriage are holy and good (Heb. 13:4). God encourages sexual relations and warns against the temptations that may arise from deprivation or cessation.
2. Pleasure in sexual relations (like pleasure in eating or in the performance of other bodily functions) is not forbidden, but rather assumed when Paul writes that the bodies of both parties belong to one another (cf. also Prov. 5:18, 19 and the Song of Solomon).
3. Sexual pleasure is to be regulated by the key principle that one's sexuality does not exist for himself or for his own pleasure, but for his partner ("rights" over one's body are given in marriage to one's partner). Every self-oriented manifestation of sex is sinful and lustful rather than holy and loving. Love is always other-oriented. Homosexuality and masturbation thereby are condemned along with other self-oriented activities within marriage. In sex, as in every other aspect of life, it is "more blessed to give than to receive." The greatest pleasure comes from satisfying one's spouse.
4. Sexual relations are to be regular and continuous. No exact number of times per week is advised, but the principle that both parties are to provide such adequate satisfaction that both "burning" (unfulfilled sexual desire) and the temptation to find satisfaction elsewhere are avoided.
5. The principle of mutual satisfaction means that each party is to have the sexual enjoyment which is "due" him or her in marriage whenever needed. But, of course, other biblical principles (e.g., the principle of moderation), and the principle that one never seeks to satisfy himself but his partner in marriage always regulate the frequency in such a way that no one may ever make unreasonable demands upon another. Requests for sexual satisfaction may never be governed by an idolatrous lust. But neither may such regulation be used as an excuse for

failing to sense and satisfy a partner's genuine needs.

6. In accordance with the principle of "rights," there is to be no sexual bargaining. ("I'll not have relations unless you. . . .") Neither partner has the right to make such bargains.
7. Sexual relationships are equal and reciprocal. Paul does not give the man rights superior to the rights of the woman. Mutual initiation of intercourse, stimulation, foreplay, and participation in the sexual act are not only permissible, but enjoined. Mutual rights entail mutual responsibility.

SUICIDAL PERSONS

Introduction. Two basic times for counseling: before attempt (preventive); after unsuccessful attempt (remedial). They occur in crisis/non-crisis contexts.

I. You can help in a crisis context (e.g., phone call).
   A. Don't try to counsel; this is a precounseling context.
   B. Try to get to the person for persuasion and counsel.
   C. Get pills, knife, gun, razor, etc., out of his hand by giving a manual task:
      1. "Get your Bible and turn to. . . ."
      2. "Put the coffee on and make some sandwiches; I'm coming over."
      3. "Write down these four things to do 'till I get there."
      4. "While I drive over, make a list of the fifteen most important problems you have."
   D. Have wife keep talking on phone while you go, if necessary.
   E. Call police if a weapon is involved or another life is threatened.
   F. Work toward agreement to set up counseling sessions.

II. You can help in a non-crisis context (or after a crisis has been averted).
   A. Set up regular counseling sessions.
   B. First session:
      1. Crucial.
      2. Set up immediately, to show concern; lessen danger.
      3. Ascertain something of the immediacy and seriousness of the threat.
         a. Ask "How did (put this in past tense) you plan to kill yourself?" If answer is uncertain or vague, this *may* indicate threat is unreal or not immediate.
         b. But don't count on this—take every threat as if real.
      4. Gather data about the contemplated attempt:
         a. "You must have some pretty serious problems to

have come to this decision."

b. "What were you trying to achieve through this?"

5. Talk seriously about all negative self-evaluations:
    a. "You must have some good reasons for concluding that your life is useless; tell me about them."
    b. "Now I understand why you say that you are stupid and rotten; those things that you have been doing *are* stupid and rotten. You are right."
    c. "The kind of life you've been living *should* be put to an end. You were right about that, but wrong (almost *dead* wrong) about how to do it. Let me tell you about the way that Christ puts an end to such living. . . ."
6. Never minimize the situation:
    a. "O come on, Sally; things aren't that bad" (very wrong and dangerous).
    b. "Listen, Bill, you aren't all that poor a father and husband . . ." (ditto).
7. Give hope (a key factor):
    a. By asserting Christ's ability to change a situation fully as serious as this one.
    b. By pointing to scriptural promises like I Corinthians 10:13.
    c. By holding the counselee responsible for his failure to meet life's problems God's way.
    d. By assigning concrete homework right away.
    e. By setting up a limited number of sessions (do not keep open-ended): "Well, it looks like this might take us eight or ten sessions to handle. . . ."

C. Session in the future:
    1. Handle as any other counseling sessions.
    2. Make yourself available for any emergency phone calls.
    3. Help the counselee to guard against depression (q.v.).

WORRY

I. Establish the fact that worry is sin
   A. Because it shows lack of faith in God (Matt. 6:25-34).
   B. Because it is forbidden by God (Matt. 6:34; Phil. 4:6, 7).
   C. Because it destroys the body (ulcers) (I Cor. 6:19).

II. Since worry is sin, there is hope:
   A. Christ came to die for and deal with sin; therefore worry can be overcome,
   B. By the power of the Holy Spirit,
   C. Whose instructions for doing so are found in the Bible.

III. Worry is a sinful distortion of a good emotion: concern
   A. And may not simply be turned off.
   B. It must be replaced by a proper manifestation of this emotion.
   C. Worry is the focus of concern upon the wrong day—tomorrow (Matt. 6:34).
      1. Mobilizing energies that cannot be released productively (tomorrow is not here)
      2. And leading to a tired but dissatisfied feeling (tensions, chemicals work on counselee).

IV. Worry can be overcome by refocusing concern upon today's tasks (Matt. 6:34c).
   A. Energies can be released productively (on present tasks),
   B. Leading to a tired but satisfied feeling.

V. Worry is eliminated when
   A. One makes plans for tomorrow,
   B. Submits them to God for His bluepenciling,
   C. And leaves the outcome entirely to God (James 4:13-17; cf. Phil. 4:6, 7).
   D. And when he determines each day how many trees he can chop down,
   E. Faithfully takes these down each day, no matter how he feels,
   F. And eventually cuts a pathway through the woods, with daylight appearing before long.

VI. Worry will not return if the counselee learns
  A. To schedule his daily work
    1. According to God's priorities,
    2. In order to avoid periods of brooding.
  B. To follow the schedule
    1. Rather than feelings,
    2. To build godly responsibility,
    3. And to avoid cowardly and fearful actions.

The Counselor's Topical Worklist

On the following pages, alphabetically arranged, there is a list of topics, under each of which appears a limited number of selected Scripture passages. In many ways, this is a curious list, as a quick scanning will indicate. But, to counselors, the peculiar nature of the list is readily understandable and, indeed, constitutes its sole value. It is from beginning to end a counselor's list. It is a worklist, based upon many of the most commonly encountered areas of needs, sins, and problems faced in the counseling context, together with references to key biblical passages that have proven particularly helpful in dealing with each of these topics.

Since the choice of specific Scripture portions will vary from counselor to counselor, according to his understanding and even his interpretation of them, sufficient space has been provided beneath each entry for other references to be added. In this way, by making one's own additions, the list may become a valuable personalized reference source that may be used for many purposes, some of which may extend beyond counseling interests. Plainly, the list is limited, but hopefully it is adequate. Too many topical or scriptural references would confuse the counselor who seeks to obtain quick help (perhaps at times even in the counseling session itself). Indeed, selectivity is what makes the list most useful. Since many persons have asked for just such a list, my expectation is that it will meet a real need.

Adultery

Ex. 20:14
II Sam. 11:2
Prov. 2:16-18; 5:1-23; 6:23-35; 7:5-27; 9:13-16
Hosea, book of
Mal. 2:13-16
Matt. 5:28; 15:19; 19:9
I Cor. 6:9-11

Alcoholism (see Drunkenness)

Anger

Gen. 4:5-7
Ps. 7:11
Prov. 14:17, 29; 15:1, 18; 19:11, 19; 20:3, 22; 22:24; 24:29; 25:15, 28; 29:11, 22
Mark 3:5
Eph. 4:26-32
James 1:19, 20

Anxiety (see Worry)

Associations (bad/good)

Prov. 9:6; 13:20; 14:9; 22:24; 23:20, 21; 29:24
Rom. 16:17, 18
I Cor. 5:9-13
II Cor. 6:14-18
II Tim. 3:5

Assurance

Heb. 4:16; 6:11
I Pet. 1:3-5
II Pet. 1:10
I John 5:13, 18, 19

Avoidance
Gen. 3:8
Prov. 18:1
I Tim. 6:11
II Tim. 2:22

Bitterness (see Resentment)

Blame Shifting
Gen. 3:12, 13
Prov. 19:3

Body
Rom. 12:1, 2
I Cor. 3:16, 17; 6:18-20; 15
II Cor. 5:1-4

Change
Ezek. 36:25-27
Matt. 16:24
Eph. 4:17-32
Col. 3:1-14
I Thess. 1:9
II Tim. 3:17
Heb. 10:25
James 1:14, 15
I Pet. 3:9

Children (see Family)

Church
Eph. 4:1-16
Heb. 10:25
Rev. 2, 3

Commandment
Ex. 20
Prov. 13:13
Luke 17:3-10
John 13:34; 15:12
I John 5:2, 3

Communication
Eph. 4:25-32

Confession
Prov. 28:13
James 5:16
I John 1:9

Conscience
Mark 6:19
Acts 24:16
Rom. 2:15
I Cor. 8:10, 12
I Tim. 1:5, 19; 3:9
II Tim. 1:3
Heb. 13:18
I Pet. 3:16, 21

Conviction
John 16:7-11
II Tim. 3:17
Jude 15

Death
Ps. 23:6
Prov. 3:21-26; 14:32
I Cor. 15:54-58
Phil. 1:21, 23
Heb. 2:14, 15

Decision Making

II Tim. 3:15-17
Heb. 11:23-27

Depression

Gen. 4:6, 7
Ps. 32, 38, 51
Prov. 18:14
II Cor. 4:8, 9

Desire

Gen. 3:6
Ex. 20:17
Prov. 10:3, 24; 11:6; 28:25
Matt. 6:21
Luke 12:31-34
Rom. 13:14
Gal. 5:16
Eph. 2:3
Titus 2:12; 3:3
James 1:13-16; 4:2, 3
I John 2:16
Jude 18
I Pet. 1:14; 4:2, 3

Discipline

Prov. 3:11, 12; 13:24; 19:18; 22:6, 15; 23:13; 29:15
I Cor. 5:1-13; 11:29-34
II Cor. 2:1-11
Eph. 6:1-4
I Tim. 4:7
Heb. 12:7-11

Divorce

Gen. 2:24
Deut. 24:1-4
Isa. 50:1
Jer. 3:1
Mal. 2:16
Matt. 5:31, 32; 19:3-8
Mark 10:3-5

I Cor. 7:10-24, 33-34,
39-40

Doubt
James 1:6-8

Drunkenness
Prov. 20:1; 23:29-35;
31:4-6; 23:20
Eph. 5:18
I Pet. 4:3

Envy
Titus 3:3
James 3:14-16
I Pet. 2:1

Family
Gen. 2:18, 24
Ex. 20:12

Husband/Wife
Gen. 2:18, 24
Eph. 5:22-33
Col. 3:18-21
I Pet. 3:1-17
I Tim. 2:11-15

The Counselor's Topical Worklist

Parent/Child

Gen. 2:24
II Cor. 12:14
Eph. 6:1-4
I Tim. 3:4, 5

Father (see Family)

Fear

Gen. 3:10
Prov. 10:24; 29:25
Matt. 10:26-31
II Tim. 1:7
Heb. 2:14, 15
I Pet. 3:6, 13, 14
I John 4:18

Forgiveness

Prov. 17:9
Matt. 6:14, 15; 18:15-17
Mark 11:25
Luke 17:3-10
Eph. 4:32
Col. 3:13
James 5:15
I John 1:8-10

Friendship

Prov. 27:6, 10; 17:9, 17
John 15:13-15

Gifts

Rom. 12:3-8
I Cor. 12–14
I Pet. 4:10, 11

Gossip

Prov. 10:18; 11:13; 18:8; 20:19; 26:20-22
James 4:11

Grief

Prov. 14:13; 15:13
Eph. 4:30
I Thess. 4:13-18

Habit

Prov. 19:19
Isa. 1:10-17
Jer. 13:23; 22:21
Rom. 6–7
Gal. 5:16-21
I Tim., book of
Heb. 5:13ff.
I Pet. 2:14, 19

Homosexuality

Gen. 19
Lev. 18:22; 20:13
Rom. 1:26-32
I Cor. 6:9-11
I Tim. 1:10

Hope

Prov. 10:28; 13:12
Rom. 15:4, 5
I Thess. 1:3; 4:13-18
Heb. 6:11, 18, 19

Humility
Prov. 3:34; 15:33; 16:19; 22:4; 29:23
Gal. 6:1, 2
Phil. 2:1-11
James 4:6, 10
I Pet. 5:6, 7

Jealousy (see Envy)

Laziness
Prov. 12:24, 27; 13:4; 15: 19; 18:9; 26:13-16
Matt. 25:26

Lying
Ex. 20:16
Prov. 12:19, 22
Eph. 4:25
Col. 3:9

Life-dominating Problems
I Cor. 6:9-12
Eph. 5:18
Rev. 21:8; 22:15

Listening
Prov. 5:1, 2, 13; 13:18; 15:31; 18:13

Love
Prov. 10:12; 17:19
Matt. 5:44; 22:39, 40
Rom. 13:10
I Cor. 13
I Pet. 1:22
I John 4:10, 19; 5:2, 3
II John 5, 6

Lust (see Desire)

Mother (see Family)

Obedience

I Sam. 15:22
Luke 17:9, 10
Acts 4:19; 5:29
Eph. 6:1
Heb. 5:8; 13:17
I Pet. 1:22

Peace

Prov. 3:1, 2; 16:7
John 14:27
Rom. 5:1; 12:18; 14:19
Phil. 4:6-9
Col. 3:15
Heb. 12:14

Pride

Prov. 8:13; 11:2; 13:10; 16:18; 18:12; 21:24; 27:1; 29:23

Put-off/Put-on (see Change)

Reconciliation

Matt. 5:23, 24; 18:15-17
Luke 17:3-10

Repentance

Luke 3:8-14; 24:47
Acts 3:19; 5:31; 17:30; 26:20
II Cor. 7:10; 12:21

Resentment
Prov. 26:24-26
Heb. 12:15

Reward/Punishment
Prov. 13:24; 22:15; 29:15
II Cor. 2:6; 10:6
Heb. 10:35; 11:26
II John 8

Sexuality
Gen. 2:25
I Cor. 7:1-5

Shame
Gen. 2:25
Prov. 11:2; 13:18
I Cor. 4:14
I Pet. 3:16

Slander (see Gossip)

Stealing
Ex. 20:15
Prov. 20:10, 23; 29:24; 30:7-9
Eph. 4:28

Work

Gen. 2:5-15; 3:17-19
Prov. 14:23; 18:9; 21:5; 22:29; 24:27; 31:10-31
I Cor. 15:58
Col. 3:22-24
I Thess. 4:11
II Thes. 3:6-15

Worry

Prov. 12:25; 14:30; 17:22
Matt. 6:24-34
Phil. 4:6, 7
I Pet. 5:6, 7

The Christian Counselor's Quick Reference

PROBLEM	CHECK SIGNS OF	and for INCIDENTAL COMPLICATIONS
ANGER temper (ventilation), resentment	triggering factors, blame shifting, underlying patterns	violence toward others, high blood pressure, colitus, ulcers
BIZARRE BEHAVIOR	sleep loss, drugs, organic base, camouflage, guilt, bizarre reality frame MULTIPLE CAUSES	sleep loss (cyclically caused by and causing problems)
DEPRESSION [ceasing to function]	responsibilities and interests slipping; following feelings: brooding, self-pity, guilt	guilt, sleep loss, anger, unbiblical language: "can't, no use," etc.
DRUNKENNESS DRUGS	bad associations, guilt, illegality, theft	liver problems, other injuries to body, withdrawal symptoms, sleep loss
FEAR	guilt (Prov. 28:1), past problems associated with fear	sleep loss, irrational actions, responsibilities avoided, guilt
GRIEF (loss)	complicating mixed emotions: fear, anger, guilt	sleep loss; rash, quick decisions
GUILT	VARIOUS PROBLEMS underlying patterns	sleep loss, anger, diversionary tactics
SEXUAL SIN		
1. Adultery	problems in marriage	pregnancy, divorce action, V.D.
2. Fornication	pornography	pregnancy, V.D.
3. Homosexuality/ Lesbianism	associations, places, pornography	bodily injuries
4. Masturbation	when, where, triggering factors, pornography	other pressures
SUICIDAL	guilt, self-pity, useless or miserable way of life underlying patterns	sleep loss
WORRY	daily output of work, guilt	guilt, sleep loss, laziness, ulcers

Chart to Ten Common Problems

DIRECT HIM TO . . .	SPECIAL FUTURE EFFORT	KEY PASSAGES
seek forgiveness, learn to release anger under control, toward problems, not toward persons	emergency conferences, settle matters quickly, thought life	Eph. 4:26-32; Matt. 18:15-20; Prov. 29:11; 25:28; 19:11; 14:29
take H.O.D. test (if indicated), sleep routine, scheduling — MEET EACH CASE INDIVIDUALLY	scheduling VARY WITH CASE	VARY WITH CASE
assume responsibilities, confess any guilt, schedule life and learn discipline, WHETHER HE FEELS LIKE IT OR NOT	allow no brooding, follow schedule rather than feelings, think list. Proper occupation, not preoccupation	I Cor. 10:13 Phil. 4:8
totally restructure life	cultivate proper friendships	I Cor. 15:33 Eph. 5:18
do responsibilities out of love for God and neighbor, whatever happens. DON'T TRY TO STOP FEARING	to focus on the loving deed rather than on the fear	I John 4:18
clear rubble from the past; reorganize life for future. Schedule	build new friends, change activities, thought life	I Thess. 4:13ff.
repent, seek forgiveness of God/man. Restitution if necessary	confess and forsake sin immediately	I Cor. 6:9-11 Prov. 28:13
REPENTANCE for all 4		Phil. 4:8
seek reconciliation with spouse, forgiveness from God/others involved, total restructuring of life	thought life	I Cor. 6:9-11
seek forgiveness from others involved	thought life	Ex. 20:14
replace bad associations with godly ones, total restructuring of life	thought life, work toward marriage	I Cor. 15:33
schedule, work hard, rearrange environment	thought life, follow schedule of time and activities, work toward marriage	I Cor. 7:8, 9
totally restructure life	growth in solving problems God's ways	Ex. 20:13
work on today's problems, leave tomorrow to God	thinking about today's problems, not tomorrow's	Matt. 6:34 Phil. 4:6